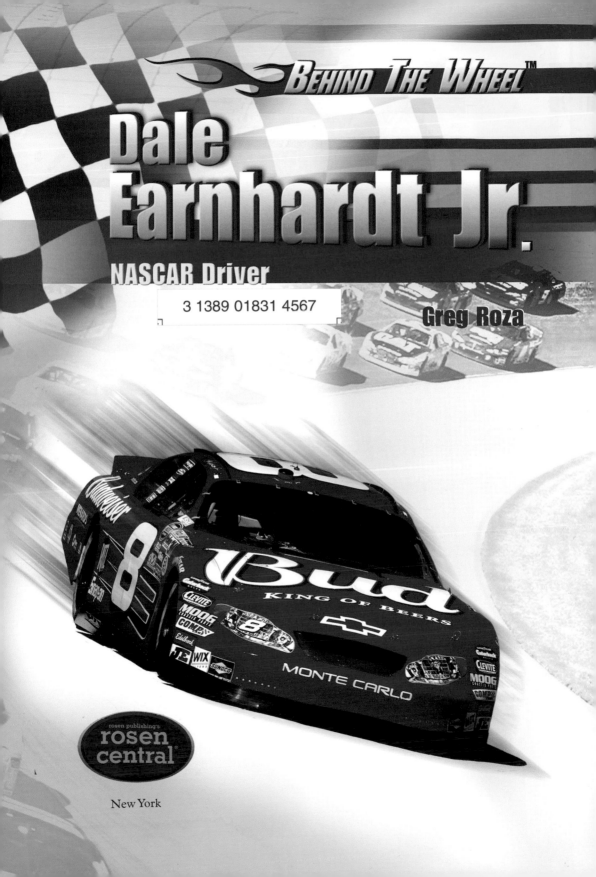

Behind The Wheel™

Dale Earnhardt Jr.

NASCAR Driver

3 1389 01831 4567

Greg Roza

rosen publishing's
rosen central®

New York

For Jessie, Tom, and Kenny

Published in 2007 by The Rosen Publishing Group, Inc.
29 East 21st Street, New York, NY 10010

Library of Congress Cataloging-in-Publication Data

Roza, Greg.
Dale Earnhardt Jr.: NASCAR driver / Greg Roza.—1st ed.
    p. cm.—(Behind the wheel)
Includes bibliographical references and index.
ISBN-13: 978-1-4042-0979-4
ISBN-10: 1-4042-0979-4 (library binding)
1. Earnhardt, Dale, Jr.—Juvenile literature. 2. Automobile racing drivers—United States—Biography—Juvenile literature. I. Title.
GV1032.E19R69 2007
796.72'092—dc22
[B]

2006021396

Manufactured in the United States of America

On the cover: Dale Earnhardt Jr. awaits the green flag before the start of the 2006 Food City 500 at Bristol Motor Speedway in Bristol, Tennessee.

CONTENTS

CHAPTER 1

It's in the Blood

Winning the Daytona 500 is one of NASCAR's greatest honors. It is the first race of the NASCAR year, and sets the stage for the rest of the season. Without a win at the Daytona 500, many drivers believe that their career is simply incomplete.

During the 2004 Daytona 500, Dale Earnhardt Jr. passed NASCAR great Tony Stewart on lap 181 to take the lead and didn't let up until he crossed the finish line. This win came exactly six years after his father, legendary NASCAR driver Dale Earnhardt Sr., won his first and only Daytona 500, and three years after Dale Sr. died in a wreck during the 2001 Daytona 500. The Daytona Speedway is a special place for most drivers and race fans, but for Dale Earnhardt Jr. it has become a spiritual

After winning the 2004 Daytona 500, Dale Earnhardt Jr. waves to the crowd. This would prove to be a major highlight of Earnhardt's early NASCAR career.

place, somewhere he feels close to his father. By winning the 2004 Daytona 500, Earnhardt distinguished himself as a truly great NASCAR racer.

Early Life

Ralph Dale Earnhardt Jr. was born on October 10, 1974, in Kannapolis, North Carolina. His parents—Dale Sr.

and Brenda—divorced in 1978, and Dale went to live with his mother. He did not know his father very well at first, but he did know he was trying to be a stock-car racer. In 1982, when Dale was eight, he went to live with his father and stepmother, Teresa.

Dale grew up in a racing family. His grandfather, Ralph Earnhardt, is on the list of NASCAR's 50 Greatest Drivers. His other grandfather, Robert Gee, was a well-known NASCAR mechanic and fabricator. Dale's father, racing legend Dale Earnhardt Sr., was an aggressive, determined racer who was known in the racing world as "the Intimidator" due to his no-holds-barred racing style. Dale Jr. learned a lot about racing from his father.

However, Dale Sr. treated his son the same way his own father had treated him when he decided to become a stock-car racer. He told Dale Jr. that if he wanted to become a race car driver he would have to do it by himself. So when Dale Jr. went to work for his father, he started at the very bottom. His duties included sweeping up the garage and cleaning his father's horse stables. He initially received very little advice and help from his father as he pursued his goal of becoming a NASCAR driver.

Dale Earnhardt Jr. celebrates his win at the 2004 Daytona 500 while his stepmother, Teresa Earnhardt, proudly shows off the coveted Daytona 500 trophy.

Dale Earnhardt Sr. *(left)* stands with fellow stock-car racer Jeff Gordon during qualifying races for the Pepsi 400 at Daytona International Speedway in Daytona Beach, Florida.

Early Racing Days

Dale's earliest memories of wanting to race a car stretch back to when he was a toddler and used to play with paper cars at the kitchen table. He also has fond memories of sitting in the grass at Charlotte Motor Speedway, watching his father race.

Growing up, Dale's interest in racing was fueled by spending time in his father's workshop with cars, car parts, and crew members everywhere. He was only 12 years old when he entered his first go-kart race. By the time he was 13, he desperately wanted to race stock cars, but had to wait three more years before he could even get a learner's permit. His father told him that he would have to be patient.

Dale began racing professionally in 1991 when he was just 17. His first stock-car race was at Concord Motorsport Park in Concord, North Carolina. He raced a 1978 Monte Carlo that he and his brother Kerry shared. Together with Kerry and sister Kelley, Dale honed his skills as a driver in the Street Stock division at Concord Motorsport Park.

Hillenburg's Racing School

In September 1992, one month before he turned 18, Earnhardt attended Andy Hillenburg's Fast Track driving school at Charlotte Motor Speedway. Hillenburg was a veteran of NASCAR who had been racing and teaching for years. From the start, Hillenburg could tell that Earnhardt was going to have a racing style similar to his father's and grandfather's. He noticed that when Earnhardt put his foot down on the gas, the young driver didn't like to let up. He even raced one car so hard, the engine exploded! Hillenburg noticed that Earnhardt—despite being somewhat small and shy— displayed a tremendous amount of determination. He had a great desire to race stock cars, and he was using this opportunity to learn everything he could from an experienced professional.

Turning Pro

In 1991, a veteran racer named Gary Hargett saw Earnhardt race at Concord Motorsport Park. Hargett had raced alongside Earnhardt's father and grandfather, and he admired the young racer's style and ambition. Hargett approached Dale Sr. about his son. Dale Sr. brushed Hargett off several times before Hargett was able to convince him that Dale Jr. had potential. After months of being pestered by Hargett, Dale Sr. relented. The two veteran drivers struck a deal.

Hargett had a late-model Chevrolet Monte Carlo that he agreed to let Dale Jr. race, and Dale Sr. would pay for engines and tires. Dale Jr. was about to get his first big break in the world of professional racing.

After competing in a few races at the end of the 1992 season, Hargett and Earnhardt teamed up in 1993 to compete in the NASCAR Late Model Stock division at Myrtle Beach Motor Speedway. Hargett believed that this short track would be the perfect place for the young driver to polish his driving skills. While Earnhardt was still several steps away from racing in the Nextel Cup Series, he was getting his start as a NASCAR driver.

NASCAR's automobiles are called stock cars. Originally, these automobiles looked the same as when they rolled off the assembly line. Cars were raced as they were sold, or racers added parts that anyone could buy at an automobile supply store.

Over time, stock cars were modified for safety reasons. Stock car drivers needed way more protection than everyday motorists. Once racers started modifying their cars, their performance improved. Eventually, the cars were "stock" in name only. Today, the bodies are nearly identical to cars seen on the highway, but inside lie high-tech racing machines.

Leading Earnhardt's pit crew, his cousin Tony Eury Jr. manufactures superior cars.

Early Struggles, Early Successes

Dale Earnhardt Jr. had a difficult time at first. The racers at Myrtle Beach were all determined to make it to division one, and competition was fierce. Earnhardt was young and still had a great deal to learn. In addition, many of the racers competing at Myrtle Beach looked at Earnhardt as a spoiled rich kid. It didn't help that his father was considered by many to be NASCAR's greatest driver. Many racers wanted the chance to knock Earnhardt out of a race just to say that they had beaten an Earnhardt on their way to the big leagues.

It became common for other racers to try to "turn" Earnhardt, or to bump him just enough to cause his car to spin out of control. Hargett allowed this to happen all season. He figured Earnhardt had to see how hard professional racing could really be. Earnhardt stuck with it, and by the end of the season, Hargett had had enough. He told the other racers that if they continued to bump into Earnhardt, he would not stop the young racer from retaliating.

Despite the constant abuse he received from the other competitors at Myrtle Beach, Earnhardt refused to give up. His aggressive driving style and determination allowed him to take a stand against other racers. Late in the 1993 season, it looked like Earnhardt was finally on his way to winning his first race. Just when it seemed that Earnhardt was going to claim the checkered flag, another racer bumped his car and caused him to spin out off the track. Hargett advised his young pupil to even the score with that racer the next chance he got.

During a race soon after, Earnhardt got his chance. He began the race a row behind the racer who had turned his car around. During the first lap, Earnhardt rushed ahead and purposely nudged his opponent's car, sending him spinning off the track.

A Promising Start

More experienced racers continued to harass Earnhardt at Myrtle Beach, but no one was able to turn his car around after that. His confidence steadily improving, Earnhardt was no longer the inexperienced "rich boy," but rather a force to be reckoned with. Despite the difficulties he had faced in his first season, he impressed Hargett with his abilities. He was a confident driver, just like his father. He was also a quick learner. Earnhardt credits Hargett for teaching him not only how to handle a race car, but also how to deal with other people.

Earnhardt competed in the Late Model Stock division for four seasons. He raced with Hargett from 1994 to 1995, and then raced with his father from 1996 to 1997. Out of the 159 races he competed in during this time, he won 3. While there were others who had better records in the Late Model Stock division for this period of time, it proved to be the perfect training ground for Earnhardt.

Great Beginnings

In 1996, when he was just 22 years old, Earnhardt competed in his first NASCAR Busch Series race at Myrtle Beach. The Busch Series, which is sometimes called the Grand National Series, compares to the minor leagues in baseball. At this time, Earnhardt was in the midst of his third season in the Late Model Stock division. Late-model cars are custom built from the bottom up based on league standards.

The cars that are raced in the Busch Series are not late-model cars. Instead, they are very similar to the modern stock cars used in the Nextel Cup Series. Earnhardt Sr. decided it was time to let his son race in the Busch series. Dale Jr. did not disappoint, finishing his first Busch Series in a respectable 14th place.

During the 1997 season, Earnhardt qualified in eight Busch Series

Dale Jr. and Dale Sr. calmly watch the competition before the 1999 International Race of Champions during the Daytona Speedweek in Daytona Beach, Florida.

races. He wanted to be prepared for his first full year in that series. He knew he would need to prove himself against the Busch Series' more experienced drivers if he wanted to advance to the "big leagues" of NASCAR—the Nextel Cup Series. Although he never placed higher than seventh, other racers kept their eyes on Earnhardt. Many thought that his racing style was very similar to his father's and grandfather's. Slowly but surely, the racing world began to take notice of the young driver.

The History of NASCAR

After World War II (1939–1945), many American manufacturers switched their emphasis from making wartime supplies to making new, more powerful automobiles. It wasn't long before people were racing these new cars. Some enjoyed racing modified versions of the automobiles that came off the assembly line, and these became known as sports cars. Others preferred to race the cars just as they had been constructed, and these cars became known as stock cars.

William France and Ed Otto, two racing veterans, came up with the idea of founding a national racing league. The National Association for Stock Car Auto Racing (NASCAR) was created on February 21, 1948. Tracks were often nothing more than sections of highway. The original track in Daytona, Florida, consisted of a stretch of highway and a stretch of beach of equal length. Throughout the next decade, race cars were gradually modified for safety and performance purposes. Only the bodies of the cars remained unchanged.

In 1956, Earnhardt's grandfather, Ralph Earnhardt, became a well-known driver. He won the NASCAR Sportsman Championship that year. His best Grand National (now known as the Nextel Cup) finish was 17th place. Ralph Earnhardt was well known for the racing innovations that he developed during his career, including safety modifications that are still used today.

Many NASCAR experts consider the 1970s to be the beginning of the modern era of car racing. By this time, great technological advances were being made to improve tracks and cars. Big-name companies began sponsoring races. In 1975, the points system was changed to the system that is used currently. Talented and entertaining racers such as Dale Earnhardt Sr. helped draw thousands of fans to the blossoming professional sport, which was now broadcast on television.

NASCAR Divisions

NASCAR sanctions three major racing series each year, as well as numerous regional racing series. Each year, there are approximately 1,500 sanctioned NASCAR races that take place at more than 100 racetracks in the United States, Canada, and Mexico.

Nextel Cup Series

The Nextel Cup—formerly the Winston Cup, and before that the Grand National—is the major leagues of NASCAR. This series features the best drivers, the fastest cars, and the most difficult tracks. The last ten races of the Nextel Cup are called the Chase for the Championship. During the Chase, the racers with the ten highest scores (plus any racer within 400 points of the leader) are given enough points to keep them permanently ahead of the rest of the racers, but within striking distance of each other. The racer with the most points at the end of the season is declared Nextel Champion.

During the course of six full Nextel Cup seasons (2000–2005), Dale Earnhardt Jr. made a name for himself as a capable driver. He won a total of 16 races and earned more than $35.5 million.

Busch Series

The Busch Series is similar to the minor leagues in baseball. It is a place where up-and-coming drivers prove that they can compete in the Nextel Cup Series. However, it is common to see Nextel Cup contenders racing in the Busch Series. It is known as the Late Model Sportsman series because the race cars are smaller versions of the cars raced in the Nextel Cup Series. Earnhardt did very well in the Busch Series, winning back-to-back championships in 1998 and 1999.

Craftsman Truck Series

The Craftsman Truck Series features modified pickup trucks. Founded in 1996, this series has become a springboard for those interested in racing in the Nextel Cup Series. It has also become a place for Nextel Cup veterans to continue racing after they can no longer compete at the Nextel Cup level.

NASCAR Points System

NASCAR competition is based on a points system. The closer a NASCAR racer is to the front of the pack at the end of each race, the more points he receives. There are other ways to earn points, like by leading the pack for an entire lap. At the end of the 36-race season, the racer with the most points is declared the champion.

Racing in the Busch Series

Earnhardt began his first full Busch Series season in 1998. He raced for his father's team—Dale Earnhardt, Inc. (DEI). The automotive parts manufacturer AC Delco sponsored Earnhardt and the #3 Chevrolet Monte Carlo that he drove.

The 1998 season began on a low point for Earnhardt. During a pit stop at the Daytona 300—the first Busch Series race of the 1998 season—he made an error that caused the driveshaft to break. Later in the same race, Earnhardt crashed his car. He finished the race in 37th place.

However, Earnhardt did not let this setback get him down. He proved that he had what it took to survive in

In May 1998, Dale Earnhardt Jr. came in tenth place in the Busch Series Gumout Long Life Formula 200 at New Hampshire International Speedway in Loudon, New Hampshire.

the Busch Series. Coming in 16th at his next race, Earnhardt had one 10th-place finish, a 3rd-place finish, and two second-place finishes in the next four races.

On April 4, 1998, Earnhardt got his first Busch Series win at Texas Motor Speedway in Fort Worth, Texas. Dale Sr. hugged his son after the race, and Dale Jr. has said that it may have been the proudest moment in his life. He felt that he had finally earned his father's respect as a stock-car driver. After a second first-place win at Dover International Speedway in Dover, Delaware, Earnhardt quickly became a crowd favorite in the Busch Series. Fans cheered for him wherever he went, and journalists lined up to interview him before and after every race.

Earnhardt was proving to be an aggressive driver, just like his father. On one hand, this helped make him even more popular with race fans. On the other, it led to some mistakes that first season, as well as several crashes. A wreck at Talladega Superspeedway in Talladega, Alabama, resulted in a 32nd-place finish and cost him the points lead. Despite the mistakes the young driver made, his determination and drive kept him within striking distance of the Busch Series Championship.

By the end of his first full season in the Busch Series, Earnhardt had won 7 out of 31 races. He also led more laps (6,055), won more pole positions (3), and earned more money ($1,332,701) than any other Busch Series driver that year. Most important, he was also the overall points leader (4,469), making him the 1998 Busch Series Champion. This also made him the first-ever third-generation NASCAR champion. The Earnhardt racing legacy seemed to have continued with Dale Earnhardt Jr., and many fans waited anxiously to see what the racer would do next.

Sneak Peek at Greatness

In November 1998, Earnhardt was invited to take part in a Winston Cup (now the Nextel Cup) race in Japan. This exhibition race marked the first time Earnhardt drove a Winston Cup car against other Winston Cup contenders. During the race he bumped his own father

Dale Earnhardt Jr. captured his third win of the season in July 1998 at the Diehard 250 Milwaukee Mile in West Allis, Wisconsin.

from behind and passed him to come in sixth! While Dale Sr. wasn't very happy about this, Dale Jr. felt that he had shown his father that he had learned his lessons well. He was on his way to becoming a NASCAR celebrity—just like his old man.

CHAPTER 3

The Big Leagues

Earnhardt had another busy and exciting year in 1999. He was only 24 years old, and he had already won a Busch Series Championship. He was one of the hottest drivers in NASCAR, and had managed to build a name for himself despite sharing the name of one of the most famous stock-car drivers of all time. Earnhardt—or "Little E," as fans were starting to call him—went into the 1999 season with more confidence and determination than ever before.

Although he got off to a slow start in 1999, Earnhardt soon claimed three wins in a row at Dover International Speedway, South Boston Speedway in Virginia, and Watkins Glenn International in New York. At the end of the 1999 Busch season, he had won another Busch Series Championship. In 32 starts, he

Dale Earnhardt Jr. lifts the trophy after winning the Napa 200 at the Michigan Speedway in Brooklyn, Michigan. This was his fifth win of the 1999 Busch Championship Series season.

had 6 wins, 18 top-five finishes, and 3 pole positions. He finished the season with 4,647 points.

In 1999, Earnhardt was invited to race in four International Race of Champions (IROC) races. IROC is an "all-star" exhibition series. Twelve of the best racers from the previous year are invited to compete against each other in four races. Everyone competing in the race drives identical stock cars set up by the same team of mechanics. Earnhardt's best finish for these races was second. But that's not bad, considering that he lost only to his father, Dale Earnhardt Sr.

Preparing for Division One

After such a promising 1998 Busch Series season, Don Hawk, the president of DEI, negotiated a deal with the beer company Budweiser. Budweiser agreed to sponsor Earnhardt in five Winston Cup races in 1999. Earnhardt raced in a Chevrolet Monte Carlo with the # 8 painted on the side. This was the number that Dale Jr.'s grandfather used when he raced for NASCAR in the 1950s and 1960s.

At 24, he was three years younger than his father had been when he first raced in a Winston Cup race. Still, everyone at DEI felt Earnhardt was ready to move up to the big leagues. Others thought he could be the racer to beat Jeff Gordon—currently a four-time Winston Cup champion. This would be Dale Jr.'s chance to prove his ability to his new sponsor, and to the world.

Earnhardt's Winston Cup debut occurred at Lowe's Motor Speedway in Concord, North Carolina, on May 30, 1999. He finished 16th out of 43 racers. During his fourth Winston Cup race at Richmond International Speedway in Richmond, Virginia, Earnhardt came in 10th. This was a major accomplishment for the Busch Series champ. His father and the other members of DEI felt that Earnhardt had achieved more than they had expected. They were convinced that he was ready for the big leagues.

Rookie Season

The 2000 Winston Cup season featured a large group of talented rookies, including Earnhardt and Matt Kenseth. Both drivers had battled it out for the Busch Series

Dale Jr. poses with his father at Daytona International Speedway. Dale Sr. had just won the first of four races that made up the 2000 International Race of Champions.

Championship in 1999. In fact, Kenseth had been Earnhardt's strongest competition in 1999. Fans were eager to see how the two rookies would do against more experienced drivers.

Despite competing in five Winston Cup races in 1999, Earnhardt still had some things to learn about competition in the Winston Cup series. Division one cars are heavier, and they feel different for drivers who are used to Busch Series cars. It took some time before Earnhardt grew accustomed to them. He soon learned when to wait in the pack and when to make a move to pass other drivers.

Earnhardt won his first Winston Cup race on April 2, 2000, at Texas Motor Speedway in Fort Worth, Texas. It was his seventh race of the season. He then took another first place at the Richmond International Speedway on May 6. Two weeks later, Earnhardt became the first rookie ever to win the NASCAR All-Star Challenge at Lowe's Motor Speedway. In addition to these exciting wins, Earnhardt was once again picked to race in four IROC all-star exhibition races. His rookie season was shaping up to be as exciting as his previous two cham-pionship years in the Busch Series. It seemed that Earnhardt was destined to win the Rookie of the Year Award for 2000.

Rookie Season Slump

Earnhardt's luck, however, did not hold out. In the second half of the season, he started to slip in the standings. Matt Kenseth, Earnhardt's Busch Series rival, began to improve. Soon Earnhardt slipped out of the top ten racers, and Kenseth took his place as the top rookie in NASCAR. Both racers were in contention for the Raybestos Rookie of the Year Award. Each season, this award is given to the rookie who earns the most NASCAR points in his best 17 finishes. Many had thought Earnhardt would walk away with the award. But due to the slump he hit in the second half of the season, Earnhardt lost the award to Kenseth.

Despite not living up to some people's high expectations, Earnhardt's rookie season was an overall success. He quickly established himself as a talented and capable driver. He finished the season in 16th place. In addition, Earnhardt had the chance to compete against his father, one of the greatest NASCAR drivers of all time. Racing against each other and becoming partners in DEI helped make the Earnhardts' relationship stronger than ever. It was truly one of the most exciting stories of the 2000 season for all NASCAR fans.

Many fans and NASCAR experts wondered how Earnhardt would do in his second season. Some thought he was overrated and would not be able to compete with others on the Winston Cup level. However, the 2001 season proved to be one of the most remarkable and heartbreaking of the young racer's career.

A portrait of Dale Earnhardt Sr. was featured on the cover of *Time* magazine less than a month after he died, demonstrating how popular he had become over the duration of his career.

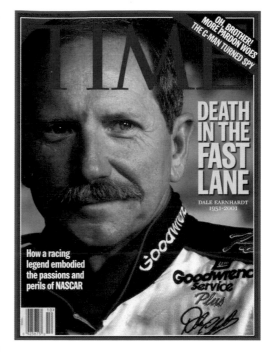

The Death of a Legend

Dale Earnhardt Sr. was a racing legend. He was also a hero to his son and to millions of racing fans. Dale Sr. had a total of 428 top-ten finishes, 76 first-place finishes, and 7 Winston Cup Championships. Dale Sr. was well known for his aggressive driving style and for refusing to allow other racers to remain in front of him for very long.

Tragically, on February 18, 2001, Dale Sr. died in a car crash in the final lap of the Daytona 500. It was the first race of the year and one that millions of people were watching. After leading the race for 17 laps, Earnhardt uncharacteristically eased off and tried to block the rest of the pack while two racers—his son Dale and his friend Michael Waltrip—battled it out for first place. Another racer bumped into Dale Sr., causing him to careen out of control and into a concrete wall. He died instantly as Waltrip went on to win the race. Dale Jr. took second place.

NASCAR fans still admire Dale Earnhardt Sr., and his trademark #3 can still be seen at NASCAR tracks, in sports shops, and on vehicles all over the country. Today, Dale Earnhardt Jr. is still listed as "Earnhardt Jr." during NASCAR races out of respect for his father's racing legacy.

Back to Daytona

Dale Jr. struggled to regain his composure in the wake of his father's death. Just one week after the tragedy, he crashed his car one lap into a race at the North Carolina Speedway, near Rockingham, North Carolina, eventually placing 43rd. The loss of his father made it difficult for him to race, and he placed very low in the standings for the next few weeks.

Despite this poor showing, it wasn't long before Earnhardt was racing his way back to the head of the pack. With a few top-ten finishes under his belt,

Though Dale Earnhardt Jr. failed to finish in the top ten for the Food City 500 at Bristol Motor Speedway on March 24, the year 2001 remains one of his best seasons.

Earnhardt arrived in Daytona on July 7 to race in the Pepsi 400. Earnhardt dreaded the thought of racing on the track that had so recently taken his father's life. Once he was on the track, however, he felt his depression leave him. He felt that his father was with him for this race, and he felt more confident than he had since his father had died.

During the race, Earnhardt drove with renewed purpose. He led the pack for 116 out of the 160 laps. A multiple-car crash forced him back into seventh place, but he fought back to reclaim first place and his first win of the season. The crowd went crazy as Earnhardt spun his car in front of the grandstands. Some people said that other racers let him win out of respect for his loss, but Earnhardt wouldn't let these comments bother him. "I want to dedicate this one to my dad," he told reporters. "This one is for him!"

Racing Forward

Winning at Daytona seemed to be the encouragement that Earnhardt needed. He ended the 2001 season with 3 wins, 9 top-five finishes, 15 top-ten finishes, and 2 pole positions. He finished the year in eighth place.

An Old Pro

Over the next few seasons, Earnhardt continued to grow as a driver, earning the respect of veteran drivers in the Winston Cup Series. The 2002 season was another exciting one for the racer. In April 2002, he suffered a concussion during an accident at the California Speedway in Fontana, California. He did not admit to having this injury until close to the end of the season, however. This most likely affected his performance on the track, although he still finished in 11th place, just one place out of the Chase for the Cup finalists.

In 2003, Earnhardt was a contender for the NASCAR championship. He had 2 wins and 13 top-five finishes. He also became the first driver to win four consecutive races at Talladega Superspeedway in Talladega,

On April 6, 2003, Dale Earnhardt Jr. celebrates his victory of the Aaron's 499 at the Talladega Superspeedway in Talladega, Alabama. This win was his first of the year.

Alabama. Earnhardt finished the season in third place in the standings, a career best for him. On top of all this, he earned the National Motorsports Press Association (NMPA) Most Popular Driver Award. After such a great season, Earnhardt's fans were expecting him to deliver something even better, and he did not disappoint them.

The Great American Race

The Daytona 500 is an annual 500-mile (805 kilometers) Nextel Cup race. It has come to be known as the most prestigious NASCAR race a driver can win. First run on February 22, 1959, the Daytona 500 has been named "the Great American Race." It is the most-watched racing event in the world. About 200,000 fans show up to watch it in person, and millions more watch it on television. It is also the racing event with the largest total payout in award money. In addition to the cash awards, victors of the Daytona 500 start the season with a win at the hottest race of the year.

Many great stories have come out of this yearly NASCAR race. It is the first race of the Nextel Cup season and usually starts off with a bang. Next to a NASCAR championship, it might be the accomplishment that most drivers strive to achieve. Despite winning seven NASCAR championships, Dale Earnhardt Sr. was not completely happy until he won the Daytona 500 in 1998, which was the 20th time he appeared in the race.

The 2004 Daytona 500

Just like any NASCAR racer, Dale Earnhardt Jr. hoped to win the Daytona 500. Winning the Great American Race is one milestone all racers hope to achieve at least once during their careers. It took his father 20 tries before he won his first Daytona 500. Many of those losses had been the result of malfunctioning equipment, a problem that Earnhardt Jr. had also experienced in a few of his first five tries. On this day, however, everything was perfect.

With just 19 laps to go, traveling close to 200 miles (320 km) per hour, Earnhardt made a daring move

and passed Tony Stewart to take the lead. Earnhardt's #8 car was running well that day, a credit to the hard work of his crew. As he crossed the finish line, the checkered flag welcomed him to his first Daytona 500 victory. With this win, Earnhardt and his father became the third father and son to each win the Daytona 500.

Dale Earnhardt Jr. leads the pack at the start of the second Gatorade 125 on February 13, 2003. The two Gatorade 125 races serve as qualifying races for the Daytona 500.

Some have said that Stewart and the other drivers allowed Earnhardt to pass them and win the race in respect to him and his father, "the Intimidator." But Stewart himself has tried to lay that rumor to rest. "I'd love to have won the race, trust me," Stewart told reporters. "I did everything

I could to still win the race. If I could have held him off, had him finish second, I would have done in it a heartbeat. But there was no holding that kid back today. Today was his day."

Continued Driving Success

Once Earnhardt had won the Daytona 500, he began to develop a reputation as a skillful veteran driver. People still liked to compare him to his father, but he was now earning respect based on his own merits. In 2004, Earnhardt had his best year yet when he won a total of six races, finished in the top five 16 times, and finished in the top ten 21 times. He finished fifth in points that year, and at the end of the season he received his second-consecutive Most Popular Driver Award.

Earnhardt had a disappointing season in 2005. He did not even make it into the Chase for the Championship, finishing a career-low 19th place in the standings. Despite this, he picked up a third-consecutive Most Popular Driver Award.

Earnhardt the Owner

In 2002, Earnhardt decided to once again follow in the footsteps of his father and move into team ownership. He joined his stepmother Teresa as co-owner of Chance 2 Motorsports. This was a continuation of Chance Motorsports, the team Dale Earnhardt Sr. and Teresa began in the 1990s to help Dale Jr., Kelley, and Kerry Earnhardt get a start in the Late Model division. Dale Jr. was the first driver for Chance 2, and won all three Busch Series races he competed in. Martin Truex Jr. was Chance 2's next Busch Series driver. Truex won back-to-back Busch Series Championships in 2004 and 2005, earning the Earnhardts two owners' titles to go with Dale's two Busch Series Championships as a driver. In 2006, Truex moved up to the Nextel Cup series and drove the #1 car for Chance 2 Motorsports.

Earnhardt also operates his own team called JR Motorsports, which he started in 2002. The first races for JR Motorsports occurred at Earnhardt's old stomping grounds—Concord Motorsports Park in Concord, North Carolina. JR Motorsports started 2006 with three racing teams, including its first Busch Series team led by driver Mark McFarland.

Earnhardt the Celebrity

Ever since his first year in the Busch Series, Earnhardt has been considered the biggest celebrity in NASCAR. He earned the Most Popular Driver Award from 2003 to 2005. Whenever he arrives at racing events, he is surrounded by fans and reporters.

Earnhardt has appeared on several television shows, including the MTV's *Cribs*. Earnhardt has also appeared in several music videos, including Sheryl Crow's

Dale Earnhardt Jr. celebrates winning the Crown Royal 400 at Richmond International Speedway in Richmond, Virginia, on May 6, 2006. This was his sixth win at Richmond.

video for her song "Steve McQueen," and the 3 Doors Down video for their song "The Road I'm On." When not racing, he hosts a cable television show called *Back in the Day* on the cable channel Speed TV, which is an updated version of a show Earnhardt liked to watch as a child called *Car and Track. Back in the Day* features footage of the early years of NASCAR and educates viewers on the roots of the illustrious sporting organization. The show also focuses on the changes that have taken place over the years. In addition to these appearances, Earnhardt has starred in numerous television commercials, endorsing products such as Wrangler Jeans and Domino's Pizza.

Earnhardt in the Future

Now in his thirties, Earnhardt is continuing to do what he does best. As always, he remains a legitimate contender for the Nextel Championship and finishes races in the top ten on a regular basis. With the guidance of Teresa Earnhardt and the support of expert mechanics and crew members, Dale Jr. has broadened his sights as an owner. He has a number of talented young men driving for him in regional divisions and in the Busch Series, and hopes to lead them to future NASCAR championships. On top of these achievements, Earnhardt still remains one of the most popular racers in the sport. All that's left for him is to win a Nextel Cup Championship, and most fans think that isn't very far away.

Awards

1998 Busch Series Champion

1999 Busch Series Champion

2000 NASCAR All-Star Challenge (first rookie to ever win)

2003 National Motorsports Press Association (NMPA) Most Popular Driver Award

2004 Daytona 500
NMPA Most Popular Driver Award
Busch Series Owners title (driver Martin Truex Jr.)

2005 NMPA Most Popular Driver Award
Busch Series Owners' title (driver Martin Truex Jr.)

Glossary

concussion An injury to the brain usually caused by a blow to the head.

driveshaft In an automobile, a rotating shaft that transmits power from the motor to the wheels.

exhibition A public display.

fabricator A mechanic who uses standard automotive parts to build a new part or product.

legacy Something handed down from one generation to the next.

legendary Very famous due to great or memorable accomplishments.

mechanic A skilled worker who repairs and operates machinery.

modify To change something from its original form.

pit stop A stop during a race to allow a car to be refueled and repaired.

pole position The best starting position in an auto race, usually on the inside of the front row. The driver with the fastest qualifying time gets the pole position.

prestigious Having a reputation that stands out among others.

qualify In auto racing, to earn the right to participate in a race based on the speed at which a racer completes one lap.

sanction To grant official approval or permission for something.

speedway A racetrack where cars race at high speeds.

sponsor A person or business that provides funds to pay for the efforts of another person or group.

stock car A standard passenger car that has been modified for professional racing.

superspeedway A race track over 1 mile (1.6 kilometers) in length.

For More Information

The Dale Earnhardt Foundation
1675 Dale Earnhardt Highway 3
Mooresville, NC 28115
(877) 334-DALE (3253)
Web site: http://www.daleearnhardtinc.com/content/legacy/
    foundation.aspx

Dale Earnhardt, Inc.
1675 Dale Earnhardt Highway 3
Mooresville, NC 28115
(877) 334-0663
Web site: http://www.daleearnhardtinc.com/

NASCAR
1801 West International Speed Boulevard
Daytona Beach, FL 32114
(386) 253-0611
E-mail: fanfeedback@nascar.com or nascar@turner.com
Web site: http://www.nascar.com/

Web Sites

Due to the changing nature of Internet links, Rosen Publishing has
developed an online list of Web sites related to the subject of this
book. This site is updated regularly. Please use this link to access the
list:

http://www.rosenlinks.com/bw/dale

For Further Reading

Buckley, James. *NASCAR*. New York: DK Children, 2005.

Gigliotti, Jim. *Dale Earnhardt Jr.: Tragedy and Triumph*. Chanhassen, MN: Child's World, 2003.

Levy, Janey. *Dale Earnhardt Jr.* Chanhassen, MN: Child's World, 2006.

Persinger, Kathy. *Dale Earnhardt: The Intimidator* (Racing Superstars). Champaign, IL: Sports Publishing, 2001.

Savage, Jeff. *Dale Earnhardt Jr.* Minneapolis, MN: Lerner Publications, 2005.

Bibliography

Adamczyk, Jay. "Racing FAQ, NASCAR Trivia and TECH Questions." Jayski's Silly Season Site. March 3, 2006. Retrieved March 9, 2006 (http://www.jayski.com/pages/faqrace.htm).

Bizzouard, Jean. "History of NASCAR in a Few Lines." Retrieved February 8, 2006 (http://membres.lycos.fr/binuxracing/history.html).

Cothren, Larry. "Stock Car Racing's Personalities & Biographies: Humble Beginnings." Stock Car Racing.com. Retrieved March 7, 2006 (http://stockcarracing.com/thehistoryof/bio/134_0305_feat/).

Cothren, Larry, and the editors of *Stock Car Racing*. *Dale Earnhardt Jr.: Making a Legend of His Own*. St Paul, MN: MBI Publishing, 2005.

Daleearnhardtinc.com. "Chance 2 Team History." Retrieved April 4, 2006 (http://www.daleearnhardtinc.com/content/motorsports/t_team_Busch.aspx).

DaleJr.com. "Dale Earnhardt Jr.: Biography and Favorites." Retrieved February 14, 2006 (http://www.dalejr.com/bio.html).

Foxsports.com. "SPEED Adds Back in the Day, Hosted by Dale Earnhardt Jr." February 2006. Retrieved April 3, 2006 (http://msn.foxsports.com/nascar/story/5263544).

Dale Earnhart Jr.: NASCAR Driver

Golenbock, Peter, and Greg Fielden, eds. *NASCAR Encyclopedia: The Complete Record of America's Most Popular Sport.* St. Paul, MN: MBI Publishing, 2003.

Grant, Paul. "Greatness by the Numbers." *Sporting News.* February 19, 2001. Retrieved February 9, 2006 (http://www.sportingnews.com/archives/earnhardt/greatness.html).

Jenkins, Chris. "Junior's Win Kicks Off New NASCAR Era." USA Today.com. Retrieved April 3, 2006 (http://www.usatoday.com/sports/motor/nascar/2004-02-15-daytona_x.htm).

JRMotorsport.com. "About JRM." Retrieved April 4, 2006 (http://www.jrmotorsport.com/aboutus.html).

Kenyeres, Catherine. "Do You Know the History of NASCAR?" Chiff.com. Retrieved February 8, 2006 (http://www.chiff.com/a/nascar-history.htm).

Martin, Mark. *NASCAR for Dummies.* Foster City, CA: IDG Books Worldwide, Inc., 2000.

NASCAR.com. "Dale Earnhardt Jr." February 9, 2006. Retrieved March 31, 2006 (http://www.nascar.com/news/headlines/cup/earnhardt.jr.bio/).

NASCAR.com. "Points System Explained." February 5, 2006. Retrieved March 29, 2006 (http://www.nascar.com/news/headlines/official/points.explained/).

NASCAR.com. "2005 Owner Standings." Retrieved April 5, 2006 (http://www.nascar.com/races/bg/2005/data/standings_owner.html).

Racing Reference.com. "Dale Earnhardt, Jr." Retrieved March 20, 2006 (http://www.racing-reference.com/driver?id=earnhda02).

Spencer, Lee. "Earnhardt's Last Race a Selfless Act." *Sporting News.* February 18, 2001. Retrieved February 9, 2006 (http://www.sportingnews.com/archives/earnhardt/selfless.html).

Stewart, Mark. *Dale Earnhardt Jr.: Drive by Destiny.* Brookfield, CT: Millbrook Press, 2003.

USAToday.com. "Dale Earnhardt Jr.—2004." April 4, 2006. Retrieved April 4, 2006. (http://covers.usatoday.com/game-matchups/nascar-race.aspx?page=/data/nascar/drivers/2004/driver8.html)

Index

N

NASCAR
  cars used in, 11
  divisions of, 17–18
  history of, 16–17
  points system of, 17, 19
Nextel/Winston Cup Series, 10,
    14, 15, 16, 17–18, 21–22,
    25, 27, 28, 29, 33, 34, 35,
    39, 41

S

Stewart, Tony, 4, 36, 37–38
stock cars, explanation of, 11

T

Truex, Martin, Jr., 39

W

Waltrip, Michael, 29, 30

About the Author

Greg Roza is a writer and editor who specializes in creating library books and educational materials. He lives in Hamburg, New York, with his wife, Abigail, his daughter, Autumn, and his son, Lincoln. Roza has a master's degree in English from SUNY Fredonia, and loves to stay in shape by participating in outdoor activities.

Photo Credits

Cover © George Tiedemann/GT Images/Corbis; p. 1 © Rusty Jarrett/Getty Images; p. 5 © Luis Alvarez/Associated Press, AP; pp. 7, 24, 30 © Robert Laberge/Getty Images; p. 8 © Peter Cosgrove/Associated Press, AP; pp. 15, 36–37 © Jamie Squire/ Allsport/ Getty Images; p. 20 © Peter Carvelli/Getty Images; p. 22 © Matthew Stockman/Allsport/Getty Images; p. 26 © Chris O'Meara/Associated Press, AP; p. 28 © Gregory Heisler/Corbis Outline/Time Inc./Time & Life Pictures/Getty Images; p. 34 © Darrell Ingham/Getty Images; p. 40 © Doug Benc/Getty Images.

Designer: Gene Mollica